SIMPLEXITY

How to Simplify Life's Complexities

Deepak Daniel
Vijay Kumar Gambhiraopet

Leading to Prosperity

Copyright © Deepak Daniel, Vijay Kumar Gambhiraopet
First published 2024

All rights reserved. No part of this publication may be reproduced, stored in a retrieval system, or transmitted in any form or by any means, electronic, mechanical, photocopying, recording or otherwise, without the prior written permission of the publishers.

All the stories are personal experience of the authors and resembling to anyone else is purely coincidental.

ISBN: 978-1-7635190-0-8
Design & typesetting by *AtriTeX Technologies Private Limited*

Dedication

*To the soaring spirit of our parents, whose winds of guidance
lifted us to new heights;
to the unwavering wings of our life partners, whose support
sustained our flight; and
to the playful breezes of our children, whose laughter filled our
journey with joyous turbulence.*

This book takes flight on the wings of all your love and support.

Table of Contents

Chapter 1
    Connecting the Dots 21

Chapter 2
    Turning Dreams into Reality... 27

Chapter 3
    Discipline, a Key to Personal Transformation 35

Chapter 4
    The Power of Let go 41

Chapter 5
    Magic of asking Help 49

Chapter 6
    The Temptation of Winning Too Much.............................. 57

Chapter 7
    Being Vulnerable.. 63

Chapter 8
    Adaptability..69

Chapter 9
    Selflessness 75

Chapter 10
    Imposter Syndrome... 83

Chapter 11
 Don't Live with Regret 89

Chapter 12
 Embracing Life's Golden Opportunities 97

Bonus Chapter
 A Journey from Chaos to Control 103

Introduction to Simplexity

Do complex problems demand intricate, convoluted solutions, or can simplicity be the key to unravelling the intricacies of life's challenges? In "Simplexity?", we embark on a journey to explore the profound impact that straightforward & simple solutions can have on seemingly complicated problems.

Is the remedy for complex problems always nestled in sophisticated solutions, or could the path to resolution be paved with simplicity? Our quest for answers leads us to a compelling revelation: the potency of straightforward remedies when confronted with life's intricate challenges. "Simplexity?" is not just a question; it is an exploration into the transformative power of simplicity.

Life, at times, disguises simplicity in unexpected arrangements, creating an illusion of complexity. Our tendency to overthink and amplify situations often distorts our perception, making simple matters appear intricate. Drawing inspiration from a mosaic of personal and professional experiences, we present a collection of stories woven together with anecdotes from our travels and encounters with renowned individuals. Through these narratives, we aim to convey valuable lessons in a format that is both simple and relatable.

Each chapter unfolds with at least three pivotal takeaways, distilling the essence of our experiences into easily digestible lessons. Our intention is clear: to contribute to the enhancement of our life by unravelling its complexities through simplicity. We believe that the secret to a better version of oneself lies in adopting a simpler perspective.

For every complex problem we encounter, this book suggests that the solution often lies not in intricate methods but in the amalgamation of simple remedies. As you delve into the pages of "Simplexity?" we invite you to embrace a mindset that values simplicity as a potent force for positive change. While we've only touched on a few of our experiences, the idea of problem-solving is relevant to all the situations we come across.

Wishing you a journey filled with the rewards of Simplexity—where simplicity becomes the catalyst for a more fulfilling life.

Best wishes,
Deepak & Vijay

Acknowledgements

Embarking on the odyssey of crafting this book on Simplexity has been a kaleidoscopic journey, and we stand at the threshold of its completion with hearts brimming with gratitude. This endeavour would not have been possible without the steadfast support of those who have woven the tapestry of our lives with threads of encouragement, wisdom, and unwavering companionship.

Our families and friends, you are the heartbeat of our existence—the silent champions who cheered us on during challenging moments and celebrated with us during triumphs. Your love and understanding have been our refuge and inspiration.

To our supporters, whose belief in our vision acted as the wind beneath our wings, propelling us forward. Your commitment to our cause has been a constant reminder of the collective strength that blooms from shared dreams.

A special note of appreciation for the remarkable Ananya Gambhiraopet, Bert Cherian, Ganapathi Iyer, Matt Hanham, Neil James and Matt Church, mentors and collaborators extraordinaire. Your insights, guidance, and collaborative spirit have not only shaped the narrative of this book but have also left an indelible mark on our creative souls.

This book is an intimate chronicle of our personal journeys, from the echoes of childhood to the present symphony of experiences. Within these pages, we delve into the profound concept of Simplexity—how simple solutions can be the linchpin in solving the most intricate problems. It is a celebration of the transformative power that small, intentional changes wield in fostering personal growth.

As we express our gratitude, we extend our deepest appreciation to everyone who has contributed to this project. Your influence, whether a gentle breeze or a powerful gust, has sculpted the contours of this narrative. Each shared moment, every nugget of wisdom, and the collective energy invested in this endeavour have enriched it beyond measure.

With heartfelt thanks and boundless appreciation.
Deepak & Vijay

Chapter Synopsis

Chapter 1 - Connecting the Dots

A routine of appreciating nature through walks, noting the vibrant colours of flowers, and capturing images. Amidst fatigue and illness, a moment of enchantment occurs as the author stops to listen to birdsong during a walk, inspiring the idea to create a video combining flowers and birdsong. This experience triggers reflections on life's lessons, particularly related to leadership, emphasising the value of accumulated knowledge, self-awareness, and the art of weaving experiences together. The narrative encourages seizing everyday opportunities to create a vibrant masterpiece, akin to the beauty of spring's symphony.

Chapter 2 – Turning Dreams to reality

We embark on a journey fuelled by the power of dreams. This is the transformative tale of a family led by a determined mother, driven not only to reshape her own family but also to touch the lives of countless other families, leaving an enduring mark on their children's futures. While dreaming is effortless, what truly counts is taking purposeful action. Along the way, we will encounter anticipated and unforeseen challenges that will put our determination to the test. So, join us as we delve deeper into their remarkable journey and witness the remarkable transformation of their dreams into tangible reality.

Chapter 3 - Discipline

Dreams ignite the journey, but it is discipline that propels you forward. Consistent discipline, in turn, forges lifelong habits. This is precisely the essence of the story we are about to explore—a father who adopted the unwavering discipline of a soldier and applied it to his civilian life, becoming a living example of its power. Dive in to discover the straightforward "six questions methodology" designed to liberate us from the digital world's grip and foster healthier relationships.

Chapter 4 - Let Go

In today's digital age, relationships often become intricate and fragile as physical distances and an abundance of distractions, facilitated by social media and virtual resources, create challenges. We explore the means to overcome the guilt associated with strained relationships and offer guidance on how to mend and reconcile our connections with both friends and family. The key to revitalising these relationships lies in the power of letting go, which this chapter delves into.

Chapter 5 - Seeking help

At every stage and situation of life, we are often confused to choose the path to take or a decision to make. From school students to accomplished individuals, we often grapple with challenges and are confused with the next step. This chapter explores the internal struggle many face in seeking help, delving into common barriers such as ego, superiority complex, vulnerability, and fear of looking weak. It draws inspiration from the insights of Manfred F.R. Kets de Vries, emphasising the importance of vulnerability and seeking support from experts. The chapter concludes by discussing perception management and the need to change how others perceive us to foster personal and professional growth.

Chapter 6 - Winning too much

Migration is a challenge and adapting parenting style in a new country, this chapter offers an insight into personal experience highlighting a clash of generations and the negative impact of an ingrained desire to win in both personal and professional spheres. Using Marshall Goldsmith's insights on the detrimental effects of "winning too much," we share a personal journey of overcoming this compulsion and adopting strategies for better communication and understanding. These strategies include not reacting impulsively, asking oneself about the true value of a victory, and learning to let go when necessary. The chapter emphasises the transformative power of these strategies rooted in empathy and self-awareness for more harmonious relationships.

Chapter 7 - Being Vulnerable

The mere mention of "vulnerability" often evokes fear and discomfort, discouraging open discussion. However, vulnerability is a powerful force that fosters connections and grounds us in the imperfect, imperfect world. This chapter delves into the art of harnessing vulnerability as a tool for garnering acceptance, authenticity, and support from individuals, transcending cultural boundaries. It unravels the transformative potential of embracing vulnerability in our interactions.

Chapter 8 - Adaptability

The chapter reflects on our family's migration journey, emphasising the challenges, triumphs, and transformations. It explores the adaptability required, especially for the child, and the leadership role assumed by my wife. Embracing preparation, unity, and a positive perspective, the family turned challenges into opportunities for growth. The narrative sees migration as a profound metamorphosis, shaping the family into a more resilient and interconnected unit.

Chapter 9 - Selflessness

We celebrate the noblest of professions, teaching and to honour the teachers, India celebrates 5 September as Teacher's Day. This story is a narrative reflecting on the profound impact teachers have had. It highlights the selflessness, consistency, and commitment of educators, narrating stories of individuals who transformed schools through dedication. It urges us to emulate these qualities, emphasising the importance of giving back, maintaining consistency, and committing to making a positive difference. It concludes by encouraging gratitude towards teachers and the cultivation of a legacy through selfless, consistent, and committed actions.

Chapter 10 - Imposter Syndrome

A professional journey marked by imposter syndrome and the pursuit of external validation, drawing inspiration from figures like Tom Hanks. We navigate challenges with historical explorer analogies, emphasising the crucial role of family support in confronting self-doubt. Over time, the narrative concludes with a call to focus on strengths, celebrate achievements, and seek familial guidance to overcome feelings of inadequacy.

Chapter 11 - Living with regret

A different perspective of letting go is how an unpleasant experience can be like a monkey on our back, a weight we carry with us and how we have to let it go to avoid adverse impact. This metaphorical monkey on the back reminds us of past mistakes and encourages us to make more considered choices and be more cautious. This burden can limit our growth and potential, trapping us in a cycle of self-doubt and missed opportunities. It is essential to acknowledge and address these negative influences to free us from the constraints they impose on our actions and decisions.

Chapter 12: Embracing Life's Golden Opportunities

The chapter advocates seizing opportunities by overcoming hesitation, emphasising the transformative power of initial decisions. Drawing from a personal experience of conquering a fear of water, the author highlights the significant impact a single choice can have on one's life. The narrative encourages continual self-improvement, embracing challenges, and seeking progress for a fulfilling life.

Simplexity Transformation Matrix (STM)

We want to introduce you to a model used in this book that can help you plan and approach things. This model will be at the centre of our discussion and will depend on four key aspects.

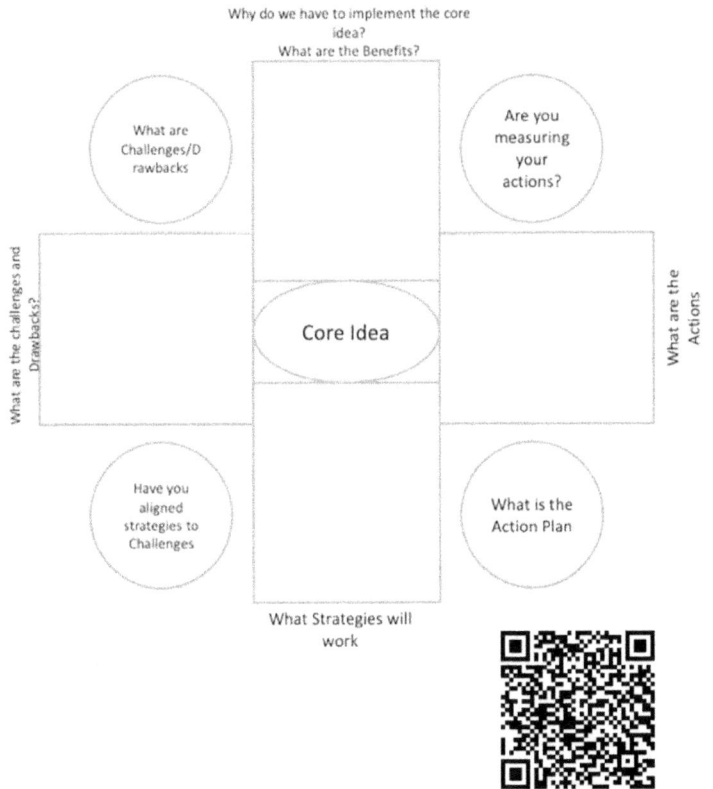

"Please scan to go to example"

1. Why is this idea important and what are the benefits? This is a crucial question we should ask when adopting anything in our lives. If we do not understand the importance and benefits of the core idea, we will not be motivated to pursue it. It is human nature. When updating the model, we must be careful and consider all the benefits needed. Sometimes, you may not need many reasons to make a change; just one good reason can be enough.

2. When we consider doing something, our first thoughts often revolve around the difficulties, challenges, and drawbacks that may prevent us from taking action on something important. Write down all the challenges in the "Challenges" box and remember that there can be compelling reasons or just one based on how you assess the situation. Some challenges may not directly relate to the benefits but still have an impact, so add them to the list.

3. Next, we need to outline our strategies or approach. These strategies should help us achieve the benefits while addressing the challenges and drawbacks. They should align with both the "Why" box and the "Challenges" box. Strategies can take various forms, such as activities, practices, approaches, or tasks. We need as many strategies as necessary to achieve our desired outcomes, overcome challenges, and obtain benefits. In our book, we recommend a minimum of three strategies or approaches.

4. Once we have aligned our strategies in an action plan, we must start implementing this plan in our daily lives. Begin with the simplest tasks until you get the hang of the process. Continue with this implementation, which will help you build your skills in the core area. You can also seek support from a coach, friends, or colleagues to assist you with your

action plan. Your plan should be implementable, trackable, and measurable.

After creating the model and its strategies, apply each strategy in your daily life with care to achieve measurable improvements. You can establish your own metrics to measure progress and the effectiveness of your actions. The best way to measure is by asking for feedback from your team, friends, manager, or family to see if they have noticed any positive changes. There is a formal method for measurement that will be covered in coaching using a tool.

Be prepared for the fact that any visible change takes time, and it may take at least six months for others to notice. Keep implementing your approach consistently during this time and make adjustments as needed.

Connect with us on simplexity@deepakdaniel.com if you need more info.

Enjoy the read! Be prepared with your stories and apply the strategy to reap the benefits!

Chapter 1
Connecting the Dots

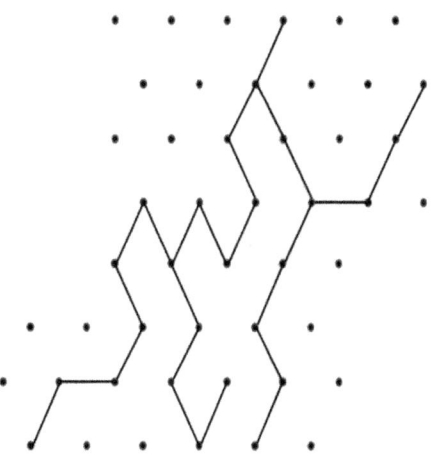

Every day, I have a special routine—taking a peaceful walk in the morning and evening. Spring has worked its magic, covering the world with various hues and colours of flowers with varying sizes. I am not a plant expert, and I do not have an interest in the details of plants and trees. What I do love are the bright and beautiful colours they bring, from vibrant shades to calming teals. These colours have their own unique language, a language that says a lot. As a nature lover, I find joy in these blooms in my own way. As a habit I click pictures of all flowers as regularly as possible.

On the 23rd of September, I went on my usual walk, but I was not feeling myself. Fatigue had taken over as I was unwell. Due to which I could not find anything exciting. In other words, my physical condition made me feel uninterested. Nevertheless, I continued my walk until I reached a corner of the park, and something remarkable happened.

I suddenly felt compelled to stop. My ears were treated to something extraordinary. It was not the sound of passing cars, distant tunes from a neighbour's old radio, or the songs from my own phone. No, it was something even more enchanting—the joyful, harmonious singing of the birds. I forgot why I was on my walk and stood there, captivated by the birds' performance. They sang with pure joy, celebrating the arrival of spring, the new leaves and blossoms, and the promise of warmer days. Perhaps they were rejoicing the absence of cold and darkness, and celebrating the present when they could fly freely and easily find food. As I was unwell, I missed taking pictures, but the joy of birds chirping, compelled me to record their songs.

As I continued my walk, the sweet bird songs played in my ears, and an idea began to form. What if I could create a video showcasing these beautiful flowers, with the birds' harmonious singing as a natural soundtrack? The idea felt deeply connected to nature—flowers, birds, and their songs woven into a beautiful tapestry. This idea sparked a fire in me, and my initial tiredness and discomfort faded away, replaced by excitement and newfound enthusiasm.

I could not stop thinking about flowers, birds, and their harmonious songs. But something else was happening; my mind was working hard, making connections, and crafting a story. I could not resist the flow of thoughts, and eventually, I had to sit down to jot them down.

During this reflection, I started to see the similarities between this experience and life's lessons, especially those related to leadership. I began to ask myself: Where is the "spring" in our lives? Where can we find "flowers" and "birds," and how does it all relate to leadership?

From an early age, we gather knowledge, from our academic studies, the professional training, and courses we undergo, the talks we listen to, or the facts and figures we grasp. Sometimes, we wonder if this knowledge has any real-world value for us. Yet, as we journey through life, especially in our professional pursuits, we realise that this knowledge is more than just a collection of facts. It becomes a source of wisdom, stored deep in our minds, ready to guide us through new experiences. Just as our first steps into any new venture can be intimidating, drawing from our past experiences can make the path more manoeuvrable.

Living in a community exposes us to countless sights and sounds—some important, some fleeting, and many just existing. To make a difference, we must develop self-awareness, recognising what truly deserves our attention. We must open our eyes to the wonders of the world while being selective about what truly matters. This self-awareness and control over our senses are critical differentiating qualities of successful individuals, like in rugby, where the players, amidst the noise, cheering and jeering, stay focused on their goal and scoring a try.

"You cannot connect the dots looking forward; you can only connect them looking backwards. So, you have to trust that the dots will somehow connect in your future. You have to trust in something, your gut destiny, life karma whatever."
—Steve Jobs

Creativity and innovation often come from connecting seemingly unrelated elements. This process requires us to be constantly ready, with our senses tuned in, to recognise what truly matters. Understanding the challenges, seizing opportunities in difficult situations, addressing concerns, and optimising processes—all of these can be addressed when we weave together our knowledge and collective experiences. And the solutions do not have to be complex; they ought to be simple, understandable, achievable, realistic, and measurable. Pursuing meaningful outcomes is our journey to succeed in both our personal and professional lives.

In the canvas of life, these three elements—experience, self-awareness, and the art of weaving—come together to create a beautiful masterpiece, much like the vibrant spectacle of spring, flowers, birds, and their songs. These opportunities surround us every day. By harnessing our experiences, sharpening our self-awareness, and skilfully weaving the threads of opportunities, we can create our own spring at any time and place. As we seek simple solutions to complex challenges, this story lights the way to success and inspires us to embrace the beauty of life's symphony.

Enjoy the video on the above topic: https://www.youtube.com/watch?v=Zz8PibaS8ZA

Exercise: Use this STM framework to define your path to find your own spring.

Worksheet

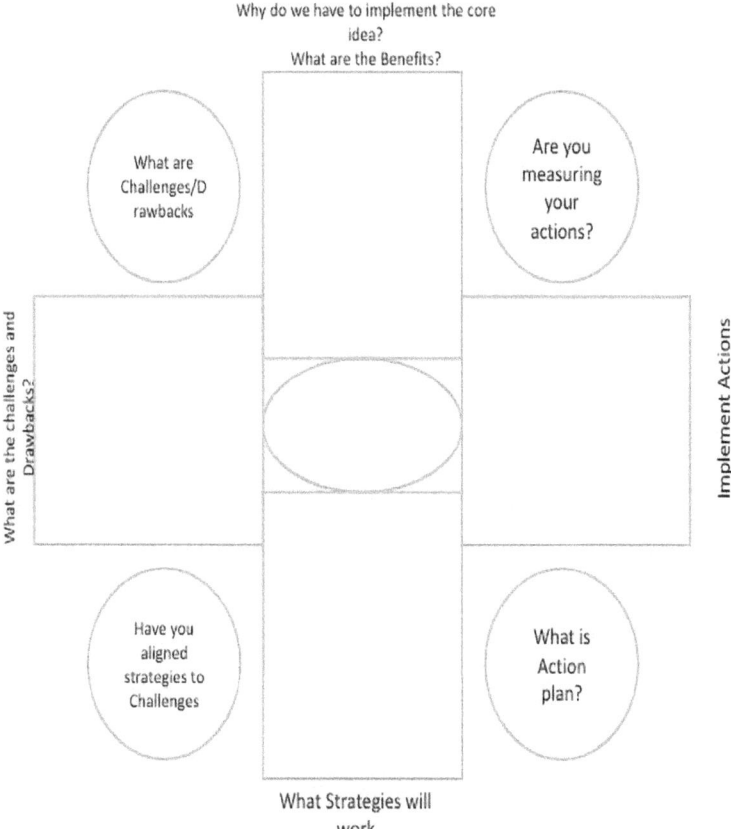

"Please scan to go to example"

Connecting the Dots

Chapter 2
Turning Dreams into Reality

In a remote Indian village, an extraordinary story unfolds—a tale of love, sacrifice, and triumph. This narrative chronicles the journey of a young woman and a soldier who defied societal norms to pursue their dreams. Despite facing numerous challenges, including mistreatment by landlords, a lack of family history, and societal bias, they were unwavering in their determination to provide a better future for their family.

Both the young woman and her husband worked in government service, which often led to transfers to different places. Their jobs were far from lucrative, resulting in a modest lifestyle. However, their aspirations extended beyond mere survival; they longed for their own home and a higher social status for their family. The young woman, a dedicated healthcare worker, bore the brunt of criticism and derogatory comments, while her husband, a retired soldier, focused on improving their lives.

Their relentless determination and unyielding pursuit of their dreams led to success. They made sacrifices, including parting with their family gold and incurring loans, to achieve their ultimate goal: homeownership. Their actions were not self-centred; they inspired their three sons, who, in the face of adversity and financial hardships, became accomplished individuals in various fields.

The family's remarkable journey underscores the transformative power of dreams, strategies, and, most importantly, action. It serves as a vivid reminder that dreams, when left unrealised due to inaction, remain mere figments of the imagination. Through their story, we learn valuable lessons about leadership and effective problem-solving.

The family's journey can be dissected into three distinct phases of action: Immediate, Short-term, and Long-term.

Immediate Action: This phase requires us to align our current actions with our dreams. Just as Rome was not built in a day, dreams demand meticulous planning and strategy. We must assess our actions to gauge their impact. Should we discontinue activities that do not contribute positively? Should we initiate endeavours currently lacking in our series? Or should we continue actions that propel us closer to our dream? It is vital to understand that inaction, too, constitutes a form of action, and we must evaluate its role in our pursuit of our dreams.

Short-term Goals: Delays in action can obstruct the realisation of short-term goals. In this context, "short-term" refers to a two-year span, divided into eight quarters. Each quarter must be characterised by goals that propel us closer to our short-term aspirations. These goals should be structured so that if an objective remains unmet within a month, we redouble our efforts to achieve it within the quarter. Major tasks should be broken down into smaller, more manageable components to ensure their timely completion.

Long-term Aspirations: Long-term goals hinge on the objectives we aim to fulfil. Take, for example, the desire to purchase a second-hand car for daily commuting. While this may seem straightforward, it entails multifaceted considerations: What will the cost be in five years? How will the necessary funds be accumulated? Does our current job suffice, or must we seek new opportunities? The couple's vision was to provide their children with a path to a professional course, the highest levels of education available at the time. Their meticulous planning encompassed various aspects, from selecting schools to arranging accommodations. Such planning, in a fast-paced world filled with distractions, can be challenging, but the family's unwavering determination pushed them forward. It took them eight long years to achieve their dream of owning a piece of land and building their own home, a testament to their dedication.

A few pointers distilled from the story towards achieving dreams:

The Power of Action: Dreams without action are like a ship without a rudder—adrift and directionless. The family's collective action formed the foundation of their success. This underscores the paramount importance of taking action.

> "Dreams without goals are just dreams and they ultimately fuel disappointment."
> –Denzel Washington

Immediate, short-term, and long-term goals must not remain mere aspirations; they must manifest in actions. The effectiveness of actions is determined by individual persistence and the extent of effort expended. Action begets results, and each action uniquely contributes to the ultimate outcome.

Consistency: Action cannot be sporadic; it demands unwavering consistency. The family understood the importance of purposeful, daily action. Their relentless pursuit of their dream necessitated ongoing assessment and adjustment. Were the children studying effectively? Was the environment conducive to their learning? Should changes be made to established routines or behaviours? Achieving physical fitness mirrors the concept of consistency—results do not manifest in a week but gradually over months and years. The constancy of effort is crucial for yielding results.

Overcoming Challenges: Action often entails confronting challenges head-on. The family's actions, including the sale of their gold and incurring loans, were not taken lightly; they were calculated strategic moves to fulfil their dream. Challenges come in various forms and may evoke feelings of frustration or doubt. We may question why we are chosen to face such trials. These tests probe our patience, energy, and endurance. Remaining steadfast amid adversity can be strenuous. The family in this narrative encountered numerous opportunities to falter or grow complacent, yet they persevered in their pursuit of improvement. Challenges were like ice cubes dissolving in water over time.

Giving Back: The family's actions extended beyond personal gain. The lady's role as a healthcare worker was not merely employment; it was service to her community. Her actions inspired her children to reciprocate, imparting the true essence of service without expectations. Giving back should be a way of life, transcending mere gestures. The worth lies not solely in monetary contributions but in the time and effort dedicated to causes or individuals. What endures in memory is not the money received but the time invested. The number of people who turned up for the lady and her husband's funerals was a testimony of their give back and the appreciations received from the benefactors owing their commitment to giving back to the community over 20 years.

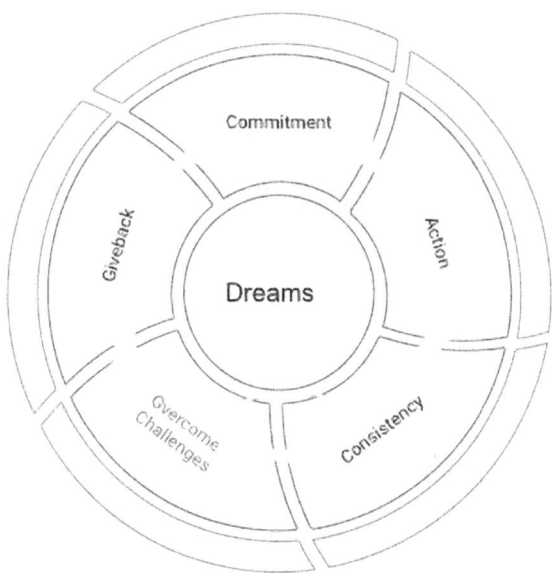

Today, the lady's children have blossomed into accomplished individuals, each a result of enduring synergy of dreams, strategies, and actions. Their triumphs reflect not only personal growth but also their capacity to effect positive change in their communities.

In conclusion, this extraordinary family's saga furnishes us with invaluable leadership insights and problem-solving acumen.

It serves as a vivid reminder that dreams devoid of action are mere figments of the imagination. Regardless of the adversities we confront or the challenges we encounter, with determination, focus, and adaptability, we can achieve greatness.

Drawing inspiration from this remarkable odyssey, let us contemplate our own dreams and aspirations. The clarion call to action is unambiguous:

Share Your Vision: Articulate your dreams openly with those who support your vision. Leadership often commences with effective goal communication. Public declaration garners support, fuelling our desire to achieve.

Strategise Deliberately: Craft both short-term and long-term strategies congruent with your dreams. Notably, immediate action should be instantaneous when required, reflecting a change in behaviour or activity. Identifying such immediate actions propels motivation toward short-term and long-term goals.

Commit to Action: Pursue consistent, purposeful action toward your leadership objectives. Recognise the profound impact your journey can have on others and your community.

As we embark on our leadership journeys, let us remember that this family's story underscores the enduring potency of the human spirit. Examples abound are all around us, especially within middle-class households, where daily activities serve a purpose and hold significance. We must decode these strategies. Within each of us resides untapped leadership potential, awaiting release through determination, resilience, and an unwavering faith in the beauty of our dreams.

Turning Dreams into Reality

May their odyssey inspire us, and may our lives testify to the limitless prospects that unfurl when dreams unite with unwavering action. The canvas of your leadership awaits, and it is your prerogative to paint the masterpiece of your dreams—one stroke of purposeful action at a time. It is a journey embarked upon simply, one step at a time, where 500 words a day can yield a book, and 20 minutes of exercise can fashion a healthier existence. These simple actions pave the way for the realisation of our dreams, and they furnish us with the ability to inspire our loved ones to dream as well.

Exercise: Use this STM framework to start painting the masterpiece of your dreams.

Worksheet

"Please scan to go to example"

Turning Dreams into Reality

Chapter 3
Discipline, a Key to Personal Transformation

In the serene and unassuming life of a veteran, every day was a testament to discipline. His routine, meticulously crafted and precisely executed, painted the picture of unwavering commitment. Each morning, the house would awaken to the aroma of freshly brewed coffee, a simple yet heartfelt gesture that set the tone for the day. But it was not just about the morning rituals; it was about the choreography of his entire day.

Sundays, in particular, became a showcase of discipline that few could match. Post-sunrise, the newspapers were devoured, and a simple yet cherished Bedi, a local delicacy, was savoured. Then began the carefully orchestrated journey to the meat market, a weekly pilgrimage that spoke volumes about his commitment to routine.

Yet, it was not the morning or the market trips that held the most profound lesson in discipline. It was the clockwork precision of his post-lunch hours that harboured the true essence. At precisely 10:30 AM, shoes were meticulously shined, sometimes even extended to the children's footwear. The room would be tidied, a preparatory act preceding the lunchtime routine. Then, with a glass of water in hand, he would retreat to his room, only to reemerge for lunch. Following the midday meal, he would slip back into his room for a rejuvenating nap, a haven of tranquillity amidst the day's relentless rhythm.

The evening sun at 4 PM would breathe new life into him. Coffee would warm his hands as he methodically ironed clothes for the week ahead. His children, mirroring his discipline, had already seen to their school uniforms. Following this, he would venture out to meet friends, engaging in leisurely games of carrom board or chess, all while sharing a few more Bedis and cups of tea. His return home, as dependable as the setting sun, marked the transition into a simple dinner and a tranquil night's sleep that harboured no room for restlessness.

His disciplined routine, a testimony to simplicity and consistency, extended far beyond the personal realm. A stern message greeted visitors at his office: "If you don't have a purpose here, don't stay." His ethos was clear—discard activities that did not add value.

In his mind, discipline was not just a trait; it was a transformative force. His approach to any problem, be it personal or professional, started from a place of simplicity and consistency. His solutions were anchored in the core of discipline. He was not a perfectionist; he was simply disciplined. His behaviours, unpretentious and pragmatic, attracted people to engage, work, and spend time with him.

This discipline was not just a part of his life; it became a legacy, a legacy that spoke volumes to his children. His unwavering routine stood as a testament to the power of discipline. His children did not learn to read the clock from numbers; they learned it from his actions. His legacy was not about admonitions or scolding, but about setting an example for his children to carry forward.

> "Discipline is the bridge between the goals and Accomplishment."
> –Jim Rohn

The challenge of changing habits often feels insurmountable, especially in today's digital age. Digital distractions infiltrate our lives, encroaching on our routines and disrupting our productivity. Despite understanding the importance of disconnecting from screens before sleep, adherence to this advice often falters.

The veteran's belief in avoiding activities that lack value was a simple dictum: "If you don't have anything, don't do it here." The cumulative impact of seemingly inconsequential acts, particularly in the digital sphere, can overshadow expectations. Limiting social media usage became a personal strategy for enhancing productivity.

A poignant observation came during a stay with a family member—an employee at a multinational corporation. His lengthy, repetitive phone calls consumed significant chunks of his day, leaving him with minimal personal time. A simple intervention that reframed the conversations led to drastically reduced call durations and an increased sense of control over personal time.

This experience highlighted a prevalent tendency in professional environments—a tendency to over-explain and feel the need to provide extensive details. Embracing the strength in admitting not knowing everything and seeking concise, focused conversations revolutionised efficiency.

The observation of successful leaders further unveiled patterns in their approaches to success. Planning, compliance, accountability, follow-up, and measurements emerged as quintessential elements in their journeys.

Implementing Marshall Goldsmith's Daily Six Questions spreadsheet presented a transformative method to track behavioural change. It required self-accountability and the humility to confront personal shortcomings, ultimately leading to remarkable transformations over time.

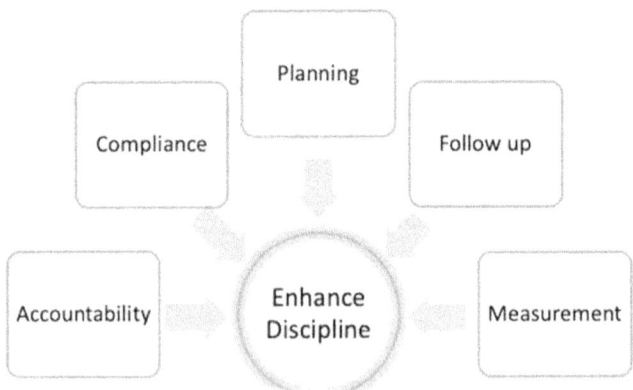

Discipline, a Key to Personal Transformation

Discipline became a crucial quality observed in leaders worldwide. It was not about seeking perfection but integrating discipline into everyday life. Small habits like making the bed or organising personal spaces became the catalyst for significant change.

The journey to discipline was not a road of complexity but one of simplicity. The transformation that discipline offered was not just personal but paved the way for professional success. It was not just about individual discipline but a collective embodiment in our habits and routines, leading us to our best versions.

Exercise: Please use the STM model below to add discipline to your own journey.

Worksheet

"Please scan to go to example"

Discipline, a Key to Personal Transformation

Chapter 4
The Power of Let go

On February 22nd, 2023, a day etched into my memory, my world was shaken to its core. It marked the moment I had to bid farewell to my cousin, aged 54, as he embarked on his journey to the great beyond. Our shared history woven through the years of growing up, side by side, forming a bond unbreakable, rooted in friendship, mutual understanding, and profound respect.

As we gathered to say our goodbyes, a shadow loomed over our shared past—a shadow cast by five years of silence, misunderstanding, and differences. What had caused this rift between us? How had a seemingly trivial family matter managed to tear us apart? Those five years, a tenth of our lives, were marred by missed opportunities, unexperienced shared moments, and withheld mutual support.

Family conflicts, particularly in close quarters, can be like dormant volcanoes, waiting for the slightest tremor to erupt into destructive conflict. In our case, proximity and familiarity bred contempt. Despite my cousin being older, false pride poisoned my thoughts, convincing me of my superiority and inadvertently fuelling the growing divide.

In the digital age, our interconnectedness often suffers. We have become accustomed to sending hastily typed messages, neglecting the profound importance of genuine conversation. How many times have we considered calling a friend or family member, only to succumb to the whirlwind of daily life, letting weeks and months slip by without that meaningful connection?

How often do misunderstandings darken our judgments, preventing the growth of the relationships that mean the most to us? When I realised that I am in a situation that I have to live the rest of my life filled with guilt for not reconciling with my cousin and cannot do anything to bring back the peace to my life, it will always remain as a hole in my relationship with my cousin.

The challenges of maintaining connections extend beyond family and friends. In the professional realm, with remote work and distributed teams, camaraderie and mental support are dwindling. Colleagues who once built lasting friendships now find themselves navigating a sea of uncertainty, where a small misunderstanding can escalate into a serious divide.

But let us return to the story of reconciliation. I recall a particularly trying period involving childhood friends who had grown up together. We were more than friends; we were family. Our journey began in kindergarten, and now, in our middle years, an unexpected shift occurred.

One among us began to withdraw, excuses replacing reasons to meet, and availability for gatherings dwindling. It was a subtle drift that left us bewildered and hurt. What has changed? Why was our dear friend slipping away?

As time passed, the gap between us grew wider, until it became an unspoken chasm. We could not let this divide persist. It was a choice between allowing our bond to wither or attempting to bridge the gap. So, with empathy and love, we decided to confront the growing distance head-on.

"Letting go is the willingness to change your beliefs in order to bring more peace and joy into your life instead of holding onto beliefs that bring pain and suffering."
– Hal Tipper

We each took our friend aside for candid, heartfelt conversations, seeking to understand what had caused this rift. It was an exploration of emotions, an attempt to unearth the hidden struggles beneath the surface. These conversations were painful but healing. They led us to a place of empathy, understanding, and, most importantly, reconciliation.

Through these talks, we appreciated the depth and complexity of our feelings. We acknowledged our roles in the situation, the unintentional actions that had hurt our friend. Slowly but surely, we began the journey of rebuilding our camaraderie, thread by thread.

The Power of Let go

My voyage into reconciliation, whether with my cousin or my friends, illuminated the profound power of letting go. It was not merely about setting aside grudges or forgiving past slights. It was about embracing the pain of estrangement and understanding the consequences of a life without those we care about.

Imagine a world without a loved one — their laughter, wisdom, and shared experiences all gone. Putting these thoughts into words is heart-wrenching. It forces us to confront the depths of our hurt over seemingly trivial matters. If only I had continued to speak to my cousin, we could have created countless cherished memories together. If we had not let our friend drift away, we would have engaged in numerous discussions and embarked on memorable journeys during that difficult period.

This journey taught me that reconciliation hinges on understanding the sheer joy of togetherness — the delight of sharing meaningful moments, the warmth of love and care, the happiness of simply being in each other's company. Once we truly grasp this, reconciliation becomes an innate choice, a path to which we are naturally drawn.

Another invaluable lesson I learned is the power of letting go of blame. Our instinctive reaction is often to point fingers, laying blame on others. Yet, this approach only plunges us deeper into negativity, erecting barriers between us and those we care about. We often forget that the other person may be wrestling with similar emotions, their experiences mirroring our own.

Instead of assigning blame to individuals, consider shifting the blame to the situation itself. Recognise that it is a challenging moment, not a reflection of someone's character. By reevaluating the situation, we can find a path to resolution, rebuild trust, and avoid unnecessary conflicts.

Silence, too, plays a crucial role in this journey. Not every battle requires confrontation. Sometimes, the most potent response is silence. It is not a sign of surrender; rather, it is a conscious choice to avoid unnecessary confrontations. It is a testament of our self-control and wisdom in choosing our battles wisely.

Considering other points of view is equally essential. In any significant relationship, we must take the time to empathise with the other person's perspective. There is almost always another side to the story, one that is equally critical. Often, the truth lies somewhere in between our narrative and theirs. Understanding the existence of another perspective can lead to empathy and reconciliation. Giving someone the benefit of the doubt can pave the way for resolving conflicts, whether with family, friends, colleagues, or team members.

Lastly, the question, "So what?" becomes a powerful mantra. In both our personal and professional lives, we encounter challenges and conflicts. It is natural to feel offended or upset, but it is equally natural to ask ourselves, "So what?" Consider the impact of reacting versus letting go. Sometimes, choosing to ignore a situation and focusing on what truly matters can provide clarity and rationality. By adopting this mindset, we can avoid unnecessary stress and find a more peaceful path forward.

Like any transformation, these strategies require consistent practice. Lasting behavioural change demands dedication, mindfulness, and persistence. Implementing these strategies consistently over time is essential. We must consciously understand why we are adopting them and remain committed to their application. Remember, practice makes perfect. Just as top athletes and artists hone their skills through relentless practice, we, too, can become experts in letting go and fostering reconciliation.

Letting go is not carelessness; it is not running away from problems. It is a conscious choice—one made after weighing the positives and negatives, considering the impacts, and understanding other perspectives. It is about releasing the grip of ego and pride to embrace the beauty of shared moments.

In the midst of my journey of reconciliation, I discovered that these strategies were not just tools for mending relationships; they transformed me into a better person. As I reflected on these lessons, I realised that the tumultuous year of 2020 had brought us face to face with the fragility of our systems and our lives. It was a stark reminder to recalibrate our perspectives, to prioritise what truly matters.

As we navigate the complex journey of our relationships in our lives, let us remember the profound power of letting go. It is a power that can open doors to reconciliation, personal growth, and a life that is more enriching and fulfilling than we could have ever imagined.

Exercise: Build your own let go model.

Worksheet

"Please scan to go to example"

The Power of Let go

Chapter 5
Magic of asking Help

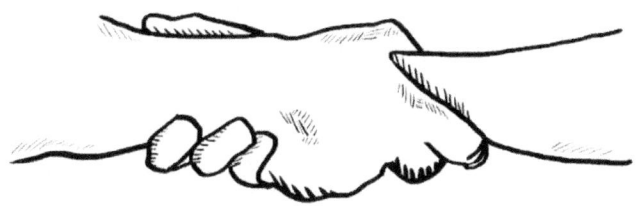

In June 2023, my attention was captured by the enthralling cricket Test Championship clash between Australia and India. This gripping five-day spectacle unfolded from the 7th to the 11th of June in the United Kingdom, ultimately culminating in Australia's triumph. As an ardent cricket enthusiast, my heart pained witnessing the Indian cricket team's lacklustre performance throughout the match, a sentiment amplified by my deep-rooted passion for the sport.

Various factors contributed to the team's struggles on the pitch. Foremost among them was their evident lack of preparation for the championship. Additionally, the players, visibly fatigued from the recently concluded Indian Premier League (IPL), grappled with avoidable errors that were keenly observed by the astute Sunil Gavaskar during the matches.

However, it was Gavaskar's post-game interview that left an indelible mark on me. His words lingered long after the final wicket had fallen. Gavaskar made a poignant observation that none of the Indian cricket team members sought his advice or assistance, despite his wealth of knowledge and experience. What struck me even more was the stark contrast: three cricketing legends—Rahul Dravid, VVS Laxman, and Sachin Tendulkar, boasting a collective tally of over 70,000 runs in international cricket—had consistently sought Gavaskar's guidance in the past. This raised the question: what compelled them to seek help, and could an external perspective, like that of Rahul Dravid as a coach, have steered the players toward a different mindset?

This revelation prompted profound reflection on why accomplished individuals often struggle to seek assistance. What if they did? What impact could it have on their path to success?

Have you ever experienced this internal struggle? Despite our inherent inclination as social beings to both offer and receive support, many of us wrestle with the idea of reaching out for help. Over time, this reluctance can sow seeds of unhappiness and resentment. Moreover, the evolving landscape of remote work has exacerbated challenges associated with seeking help from colleagues.

While self-reliance is undoubtedly commendable, recognising when we are pushing our limits and being open to seeking help are equally essential for personal and professional fulfilment. However, understanding why many of us grapple with this is crucial. Let us explore some common barriers that often hinder us from asking for assistance:

Magic of asking Help

1. EGO: "What would people think? What will my parents think? I am the best in the business."
2. Superiority Complex: Sometimes, we overestimate our capabilities and assume we have all the answers.
3. Vulnerability: The reluctance to display vulnerability often stems from our desire to project unwavering strength as leaders.
4. Fear of Looking Weak: Asking for help can be unfairly interpreted as a personal weakness, a perspective we need to change.
5. Fear of Losing Control: The fear of losing control over a situation or us can make seeking help seem daunting.
6. Fear of Rejection: The act of seeking assistance can come with the fear of not being accepted or valued by others.
7. Superstition: Relying on superstitions may hinder our progress and decision-making.
8. Overconfidence: Overconfidence can sometimes blind us to our limitations.
9. Imposter Syndrome: Even high achievers can grapple with imposter syndrome, deterring them from seeking help. (Refer Chapter 10)
10. Status Quo: Stubbornly adhering to the status quo can hinder progress and eventual solutions.

In our exploration of the significance of seeking support, we draw inspiration from the experiences and insights shared by Manfred F.R. Kets de Vries, the Distinguished Clinical Professor of Leadership Development and Organisational Change at INSEAD, in his July 2023 article in the Harvard Business Review titled "Why It's So Hard to Ask for Help?"

Vulnerability: The Courage to Admit You Need Help

One of the most challenging barriers to asking for help is the vulnerability it entails. It is not easy to admit that we do not have all the answers or that we need assistance. Many successful leaders have faced failures in their lives because they were hesitant to embrace their vulnerability. However, vulnerability is not a sign of weakness but an indication of courage. In Brené Brown's "The Power of Vulnerability," she emphasises that dropping the armour that shields us from vulnerability can open us up to experiences that bring purpose and meaning to our lives. Recognising our vulnerability can be the starting point for innovation, adaptability, accountability, and visionary leadership. To overcome this barrier, we must first identify the "armour" that makes us shut down and work on changing it. As we do so, we become better equipped to ask for help and become leaders who inspire trust and comfort in those around us.

Talk to an Expert: Trusting Professionals for Support

In today's digital age, it is common for us to turn to the internet for advice on various issues, from health concerns to relationship problems. However, relying solely on internet searches, often referred to as "Dr. Google," can lead to misunderstandings and unnecessary anxiety. Seeking advice from qualified experts who have the knowledge and experience to provide personalised guidance is crucial. Just as you would consult a doctor for a health issue, it is essential to reach out to professionals in their fields when needed. In a society where asking for help regarding mental health or personal issues is sometimes stigmatised, it is essential to stand up and seek assistance. Seeking help is not always about consulting a doctor; it can also involve reaching out to friends, family members, or mentors who can listen, understand your situation, and offer their support. In the professional realm, having a coach or mentor can be instrumental in challenging us on our journey and help recalibrate our goals. These individuals can provide fresh perspectives and guide in seeing things differently.

Below, the picture illustrates how a challenging and weighty problem can be illuminated, guiding us towards acheiving our best over time.

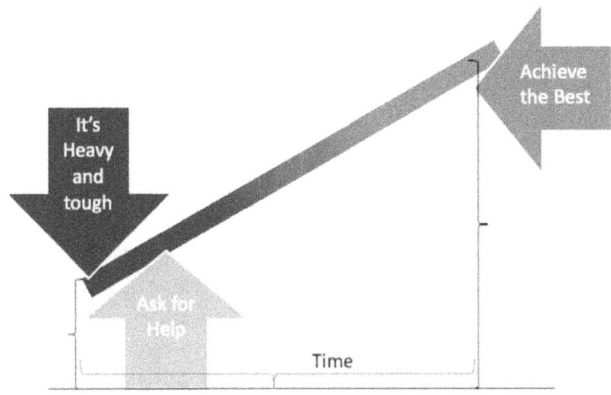

Asking help achieve results

Perception Management: Changing How Others See Us

Changing how others perceive us can be a challenging endeavour. Often, people hold onto outdated perceptions, even when we have transformed ourselves. It is demoralising when we have evolved, but others continue to see us in the same light. To change these perceptions, we must consistently demonstrate our growth and openness. Perception management takes time and effort, and it requires us to be visible and showcase our change. People's opinions change through experiencing our transformation firsthand and hearing about it through word of mouth. There is no shortcut to perception management; it is a complex interpersonal skill that needs to become an integral part of our lives.

The Power of Let Go: A Key to Seeking Help (Refer Chapter 4)

Letting go is a practice that can yield great results in life. It requires enormous courage to ask for help and to let go of the fear of rejection or inadequacy. While there may be people who will not support us, there are many more who are ready and willing to help. Moreover, we should not see seeking help as a one-sided transaction. It is not always about taking; we should also be willing to give back. By sharing our experiences and stories, we can provide valuable support to others who may be going through similar challenges. Helping and asking for help can be a mutually beneficial exchange. Seeking help can enhance relationships, free up time to focus on critical tasks, and lead to personal and professional growth.

Street Smart: Artful Requesting

When seeking help, it is essential to be truthful and humble in your approach. Do not challenge others to help you; instead, build their confidence in your quest for improvement. Clearly articulate what you need, why you need it, and suggest practical steps for those you are asking. Ensure that your request is within their ability and be explicit about when you need their assistance. Practise this skill regularly and understand that those around you are observing your behaviour.

> "Dependence starts when we are born and lasts until we die. We accept our dependence as babies and ultimately, with varying degrees of resistance, we accept help when we get to the end of our lives. But in the middle of our lives, we mistakenly fall prey to the myth that successful people are those that help rather than need, and broken people need rather than help."
>
> — Brené Brown

Team Player: Building Trust and Camaraderie

In a team environment, being a team player is vital. Team dynamics evolve through stages of forming, norming, and performing. Building trust and camaraderie within the team can create an environment where seeking help is encouraged. Team members need to trust one another and feel comfortable being vulnerable. By fostering confidence within the team, you can create an atmosphere where reaching out for assistance is natural and mutually beneficial.

Practice, Practice, Practice: Mastery Through Repetition

As with any skill, asking for help becomes more natural with practice. Recognise that people around you are watching and learning from your example. Be mindful of your approach and when, how, and what to ask for. Over time, asking for help will become second nature.

In conclusion, do not shy away from seeking help or extending it to others. Recognise that vulnerability is a source of strength, trust is a two-way street, perception management is a gradual process, and letting go can be liberating. By asking for help and offering it, we can build authentic, lasting, and trusting relationships. As Simon Sinek aptly puts it, "We don't build trust when we offer help. We build trust when we ask for it." Trust works both ways, and the magic happens when we seek assistance. Keep your doors open and be ready to seek and provide support that can change lives, both yours and others'. The results could have been different for India in the Test World Cup if they had sought the support of experts.

Exercise: Build your own asking for help model.

Worksheet.

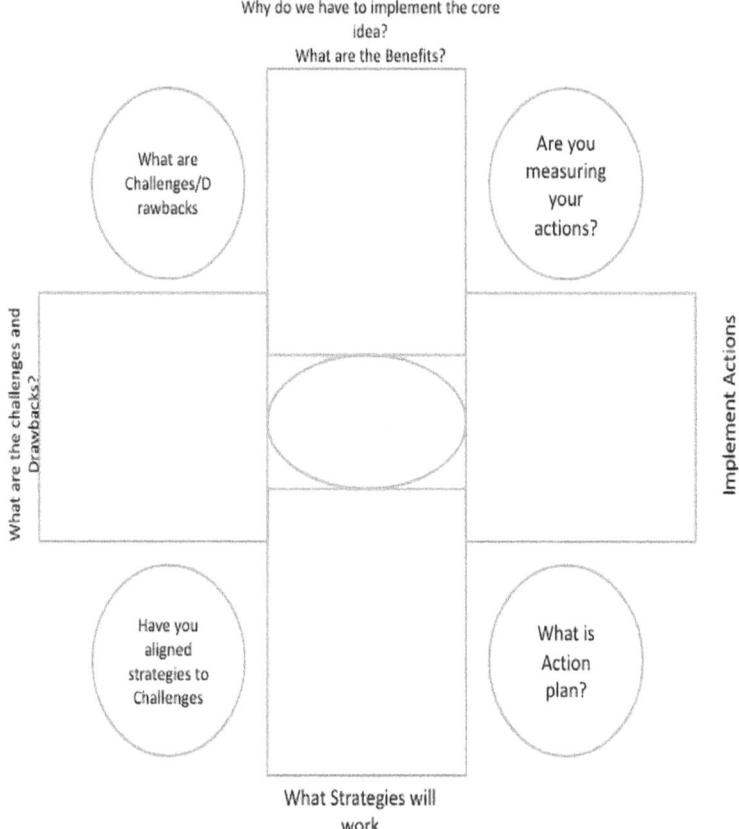

"Please scan to go to example"

Chapter 6

The Temptation of Winning Too Much

Our journey began in India, carrying our rich culture and educational values with us wherever life led. As we ventured into different countries, we could not help but view their education systems and our children's behaviours through the lens of our homeland. We often compared it to a world our children had not experienced until we moved abroad. Our story mirrors this, as we pushed our son relentlessly in his education, failing to grasp his perspective. We clung to practices from 30 years ago, unaware of their diminishing relevance in today's fast-paced world. In this clash of generations, conflicts at home were frequent, and our determination to prove our points took a toll, especially during his mid to late teens. Our household became a battleground, frustration and helplessness prevailing on both sides. Winning at any cost had become the norm, and it was far from a healthy environment.

As new migrants in an unfamiliar land, we lacked friends with whom we could share our struggles and learn from their experiences. It was amidst this turbulent backdrop that I stumbled upon Marshall Goldsmith's book, "What Got You Here Won't Get You There." His words resonated deeply with me, despite the book primarily addressing corporate challenges. I could see its relevance to my personal situation.

Marshall Goldsmith's keen observation hit home: "Winning too much" stands as the paramount challenge for most individuals, serving as the root cause of numerous behavioural issues. Excessive arguments, driven by the need for our viewpoint to triumph, reflect our insatiable desire to win. Belittling others subtly positions us as superior, seeking victory once more. Hoarding information becomes a strategy to gain an edge over peers, and even favouritism becomes a means to stack the odds in our favour.

This compulsion to win does not confine itself to our professional lives; it permeates our personal spheres as well. We, the winners, are hardwired to seek victory in important contests, meaningful debates, critical decisions, trivial arguments, and even endeavours hardly worth our effort. The relentless pursuit of victory becomes an integral part of our identity.

For individuals who are intelligent and accomplished, letting go of the constant need to win presents a monumental challenge. A compelling test, one that many unwittingly fail, exposing a deeply ingrained habit. Imagine this scenario (Test): After a challenging day at work, you return home to find your spouse waiting, saying, "I had such a tough day today..." But before they can finish, you interject, "You had a tough day? Do you even comprehend what I had to endure today?" It is a subtle competition to emerge as the most miserable person in the room, to win at being more miserable than the ones we share our lives with (Source: MGSCC)

Now, reflect upon this revelation armed with the knowledge of how deeply ingrained our competitiveness becomes as we mature and navigate life. Consider the consequences: how many evenings have we been marred with heated disputes, not just affecting us but also impacting our loved ones, children, extended family, and friends? In my personal journey, spanning 23 years of marriage, I have become acutely aware of this issue. Our experiences mirrored these case studies countless times, as my spouse and I both clung to an unrelenting desire to emerge victorious in every situation.

Consciously, I began adopting strategies to preserve our harmony:

Do Not React: In situations that could lead to confrontation or involve my superior knowledge, I have learned to hold my reactions. No longer do I react impulsively in public. Instead, I make note of the issue, review it privately, and objectively assess the situation. If it reveals areas that need addressing, I attempt to highlight these points in a manner that encourages discussion rather than confrontation. I refrain from imposing my viewpoint and strive to achieve a shared understanding, ensuring that all parties appreciate the risks and benefits of the decision at hand, whether in our personal lives or within our organisation.

> "No matter if you win or lose, the most important thing in life is to enjoy what you have."
> — Dong Dong

Ask Yourself: I have adopted a practice of taking a deep breath and asking myself, "What am I truly gaining here? Is this victory something I genuinely desire or need? Is it even worth the effort?" Recognizing this "flaw" within ourselves and working to suppress it in our interactions with others can pave the path to greater success. Often, when we are in a response mode, we hear something, and the next thing we do is respond to the comments. We are not listening to understand; rather, we are waiting to respond. This happens at work when we receive an email – our first reaction is to respond back to the sender, sometimes in capitals or with the intent of proving our point. In such moments, it is valuable to remember the advice to step away for a moment. Even if I have typed a response, before sending it, I take a brief break. Upon returning and re-reading, I often find that it is not worth engaging in that manner. The same approach applied to our case study; enjoying a great meal was what was required, not winning an argument.

Let Go: Sometimes, it is wiser to lose a battle to win the war. I have learned to let go, to yield when the matter at hand holds no significant impact on our professional or personal lives. It is easy; we are not losing anything unless it critically impacts our personal life or business. We need to prioritise tasks based on their impact. If there is no substantial impact, there is no need to invest our time and energy there. There may be an alternative approach or method preferred by others, and that is acceptable. Encouraging our teams to take calculated risks and learn from their experiences empowers them to become self-reliant problem solvers rather than relying on us for answers.

Implementing these strategies is no easy task, as I have come to realise. While the benefits are evident, the discipline required to follow a routine remains a challenge for most of us. Humans often thrive with guidance and support, and having someone in our close circle or a dedicated coach to monitor our progress and offer encouragement can make a world of difference.

Now, with my son, our arguments have significantly reduced, and the focus has shifted towards defining what "good" looks like and understanding what truly matters in each situation. I have stopped trying to win over my son; these days, I find joy in conceding and giving in to him. He, too, has changed and learned the concept of "It's okay." These concepts have made a significant positive impact on my personal life.

In the intricate tapestry of "Simplexity," these strategies, rooted in empathy and self-awareness, have transformed the way I navigate my personal and professional relationships. The path to a more harmonious existence begins with recognising the subtle, pervasive desire to win. By embracing these strategies, I strive to become a better version of myself, not only for my sake but also for those I hold dear.

Exercise: Build our own model to get over winning too much.

Worksheet

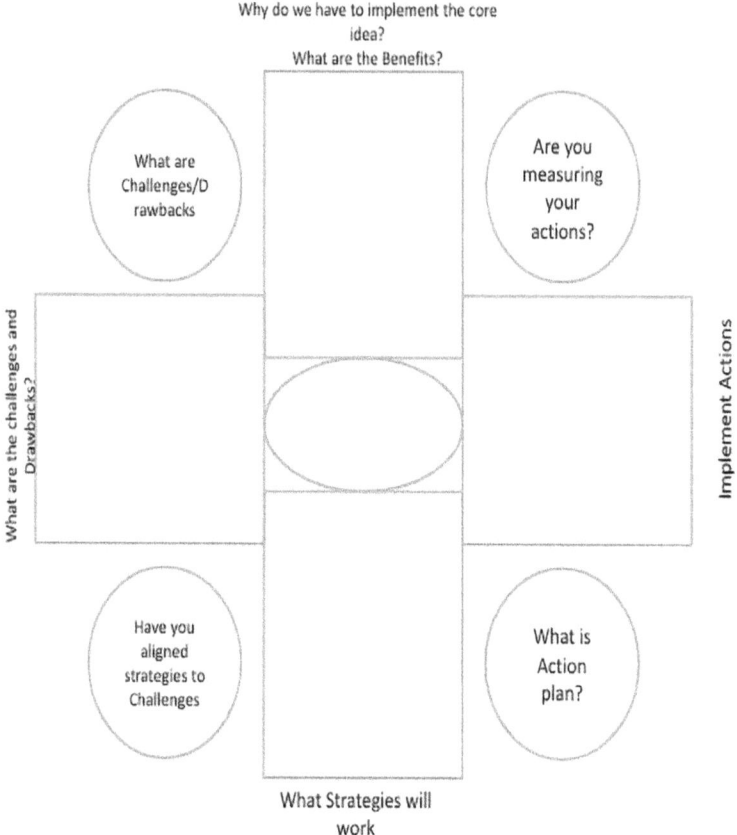

"Please scan to go to example"

The Temptation of Winning Too Much

Chapter 7
Being Vulnerable

In a world often defined by the masks we wear to conceal our vulnerabilities; the facade of strength can eclipse our authentic selves. We fear ridicule and judgement, a trepidation that keeps us from forging deep connections and earning the trust of others. Paradoxically, the very effort to hide our vulnerabilities obstructs our personal growth and constrains our ability to connect with those around us.

Parenting - Embracing the Universal Experience of Vulnerability:

As individuals, we all encounter moments of vulnerability, a universal yet often overlooked aspect of the human experience. One arena where vulnerability frequently surfaces is in our relationships and in the role of parenting—a shared encounter expressing itself through frustration, disappointment, or anger.

Proud parents, my wife and I, navigated the complexities of parenthood through the lens of inexperience. Our journey involved experimenting with teaching our daughter about the world, all while grappling with constant travel and exposure to contrasting cultures during her teenage years, which unfolded as a mosaic of laughter and tears. Trivial discussions escalated into arguments, withdrawn silence, and culminated in hugs laced with tears of repentance and eventual laughter.

Gradually, we realised the lack of parenting experience echoed in our frequent mantra, "No one taught us." Simultaneously, we faced the counter of similar inexperience from our beloved daughter, guiding us through the complexities of her teenage years. As she grew, arguments toned down with quick realisations of our strengths and weaknesses. Acceptance became the key to navigating challenges. We understood that overcoming our challenges was possible only by acknowledging and embracing our vulnerabilities.

As a beautiful chapter of our life as a family, the challenges of parenthood transformed into threads woven with laughter, tears, and moments of deep understanding. Our daughter, without realising it, became our greatest teacher. By embracing acceptance and understanding, we not only navigated the storms of teenage years but also emerged as a stronger family, welcoming the continuous growth that comes with the shared experience.

"Vulnerability is our most accurate measurement of courage."

Oprah's Radiant Vulnerability:

This story resonates deeply with the timeless teachings of the Bhagavad Gita, which underscore the importance of performing actions without attachment to the outcomes. By embracing who you are and focusing on the process rather than fixating on the result, individuals can navigate life with grace and authenticity.

Oprah Winfrey, an iconic media personality, epitomises this principle. She defines vulnerability as the willingness to lay bare the truth of one's essence. Oprah has courageously bared her own vulnerabilities over the years, particularly when it comes to her struggles with weight and body image. She has openly shared her battles with emotional eating and the daunting challenge of maintaining a healthy lifestyle.

Oprah's embodiment of Empathy (vulnerability) creates a haven for her guests, a space where they can candidly open up and share the intricacies of their lives. This is the very heart of her show's monumental success—a testament to the extraordinary power of vulnerability in forging deep and authentic connections.

Navigating Mental Health Challenges:

In the uncharted terrain of mental health, vulnerability emerges as a constant companion—an intimate aspect of the journey toward healing and self-discovery. Recognising and embracing Acceptance(vulnerability) in mental health is not a sign of weakness; rather, it signifies a courageous step toward understanding and resilience.

Amid silent battles with anxiety and depression, mental health vulnerability often remains concealed behind smiles and daily routines, demanding compassion and understanding. The tribulations of the COVID-19 pandemic have intensified these struggles, with a CDC study revealing that 25% of participants displayed symptoms of depression, and half of young adults (aged 18-24) exhibited heightened levels.

> "To grow up is to accept vulnerability, to be alive is to be vulnerable."
> — Madeleine L'Engle

Confronting depression requires delicate acknowledgment of one's vulnerability. Strategies include seeking support from professionals or confiding in trusted connections, establishing consistent routines, and focusing on controllable aspects to alleviate stress. This narrative is a testament to the transformative power of vulnerability—not a fragility but a dynamic force weaving the fabric of our existence, fostering connections, empowering triumphs, and carving a path to greatness. It extends beyond personal growth; it resonates deeply in the realm of building resilient and genuine relationships. Channelling the spirit of Oprah's radiant empathy emphasises the creation of spaces where life stories can be shared openly, free from the shadows of judgement. Oprah's show serves as a living proof of vulnerability's unparalleled capacity to forge profound connections and contribute to resounding success.

Aligned with the timeless wisdom of the Bhagavad Gita, the tale reminds us of the profound value in focusing on the journey itself, detached from the fixation on outcomes. Being vulnerable, within life's intricate tapestry, emerges as a guiding light—a robust force that transcends our perceived weaknesses, uniting us in the shared journey of authenticity and genuine connection.

Yet, our exploration of vulnerability does not conclude here. It extends its tendrils into the intimate realms of relationships, parenting, and the depths of mental health struggles. Through our personal stories and shared experiences, it becomes the bridge that connects hearts, the foundation upon which trust is built, and the catalyst for personal and collective resilience.

Being Vulnerable

So, as we stand at the culmination of these experiences, let it be a call to arms—an invitation to embrace, who we are? Vulnerability not as a liability but as an extraordinary asset. It beckons us to live authentically, connect genuinely, and navigate the complexities of life with the strength that vulnerability bestows upon us. In doing so, we unlock the full spectrum of our human experience, discovering that, indeed, vulnerability is not a weakness but a profound and radiant source of strength.

Exercise: Build our own model to get our vulnerability.

Worksheet

"Please scan to go to example"

Being Vulnerable

Chapter 8
Adaptability

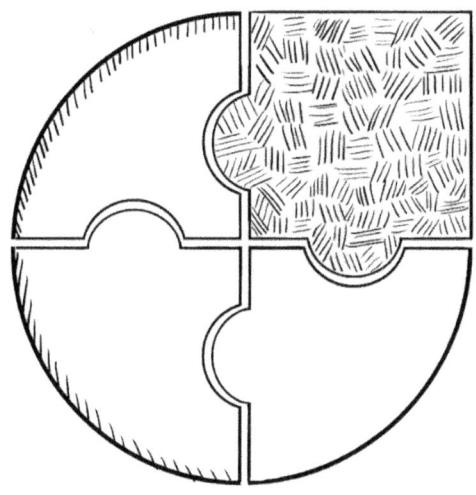

Migration—a term that conjures varied images and emotions for different souls. To some, it may evoke the majestic spectacle of birds embarking on epic journeys, soaring across vast distances in search of greener pastures or warmer climes. Yet, for my family, migration held an entirely distinct meaning, one that would take us on an odyssey of human experience. It meant uprooting our lives from the familiar and replanting them in a foreign soil, often with uncertainty lingering like an uninvited guest, pondering how long we would call this new place home.

A Whirlwind of Emotions: Our journey to a new and unfamiliar country was a maelstrom of emotions, a symphony of excitement and anxiety that played out in every aspect of our lives. It was a saga of new beginnings, a daunting feat that demanded every ounce of our resolve. Finding a place to call home, adapting to the rhythms of new schools, and immersing ourselves in the tapestry of a foreign culture, cuisine, and language became our daily pursuits. It was a lot to digest, but it was a journey we embarked upon as a family, united by our determination and boundless love for one another.

> "I'll do whatever it takes to win games, whether it's sitting on the bench waving a towel, handing a cup of water to a teammate or hitting the game-winning shot."
> — Kobe Bryan

The Brave Voyager: Of all of us, my daughter was the true intrepid explorer, navigating the uncharted territories of her new life with unwavering courage. She had to manoeuvre the labyrinthine corridors of a foreign education system, adapting to a style of learning that was a world apart from what she had known. Forming new friendships became an adventure in itself, and the need to pick up a new language or adopt a different accent added to the tapestry of challenges she embraced.

Every country introduced us to a different education system, each with its own unique intricacies and demands. But my daughter, she remained steadfast, never once uttering a complaint. She carried herself with remarkable grace, a testament to her resilience and spirit.

The Pillar of Strength: In this unfolding drama of migration, credit must be bestowed upon my wife, who gracefully undertook the roles of teacher, mentor, and guide. She was the anchor that steadied our ship as we sailed through turbulent waters. Her tireless efforts were instrumental in helping our daughter

Adaptability

transition into her new environment, providing her with the vital support she needed.

In her role as the pillar of strength, my wife not only managed the practicalities of our new life but also became the emotional anchor for our family. Her ability to maintain a sense of stability amid the flux of change and to provide unwavering support during moments of uncertainty, became the bedrock upon which we all relied. Her comforting presence turned challenges into opportunities for growth and understanding.

The Unwavering Spirit: In the grand scheme of our lives, it was our daughter who truly dazzled with her unyielding spirit. Each new chapter in her life was embraced not as a hurdle, but as an opportunity—an opportunity to explore a world teeming with potential friends, intriguing books, and inspiring teachers.

Her unwavering spirit was not just a response to challenges; it became a beacon of optimism for our entire family. Whether it was adapting to a new school, navigating cultural nuances, or forming connections in a foreign land, her enthusiasm and resilience infused our journey with a sense of adventure and possibility. Her ability to find joy in the unfamiliar and turn every experience into a lesson in growth transformed our migration story into a narrative of resilience and strength.

Adaptability in Life's Theatre: In the theatre of life, they say that change is the only constant, and the ability to adapt is a skill worth acquiring. As a family, we ventured into this unknown landscape together, fully aware that there was no one-size-fits-all manual for learning. We learned, instead, to focus on the positives, to remain open to the multitude of possibilities that lay ahead, and to craft inventive solutions to the unique challenges that greeted us on our journey. The unpredictability of migration became a canvas for us to paint with the vibrant hues of adaptability, turning each obstacle into a stepping stone toward a richer, more interconnected life.

The Transformation of Migration: Migration may lead us into the unknown, but with the unwavering support of our loved ones, it has the potential to transform into a journey of profound personal growth and resounding success. It serves as a poignant reminder that change, while undeniably daunting, possesses the power to open doors to new horizons, to forge bonds stronger than ever, and to uncover hidden strengths that may otherwise have remained dormant.

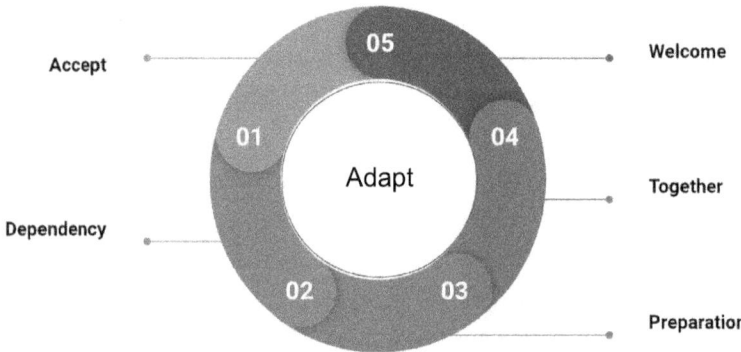

Having traversed numerous countries, in summary our journey was made possible through:

- Preparation: Mentally, physically, and thorough research laid the foundation for our odyssey.

- Adapting: Embracing vulnerability, staying true to ourselves, and welcoming the newness that life offers.

- Being Together: Amidst challenges, staying united became our winning strategy, never losing sight of our purpose.

- Leadership: My wife, a pillar of strength, assumed a leadership role; without her, our family would not be where it is today.

- All Is Well: The notion of "all is well" is relative; each culture and country present unique challenges. Shifting our perspective to making each place our own transformed the feeling of well-being.

- Pain: Just as sitting in one place for too long brings discomfort, our family, having moved to six countries in the last 20 years, carries the scars of each. Yet, as a family of travellers, we embraced the pain, cherishing the invaluable love and affection bestowed upon us by each country.

Migration is never easy; however, we can make it a beautiful experience that will teach how to live and will build a bundle of joy to narrate stories. In the narrative of life, migration stands as a chapter filled with both trials and triumphs—a testament to the indomitable resilience of the human spirit and the enduring power of familial love and unity. It is a drama of transformation, of embracing the unknown with open arms, and finding beauty and strength in the unlikeliest of places. As we reflect on our migration journey, we realise that it was not just a physical relocation; it was a profound metamorphosis—a shedding of old selves and the emergence of a more adaptable, resilient, and interconnected family. Our migration story is not just about the places we have been, it is about the people we have become in the process.

Exercise: Build your own adaptability model.

Worksheet

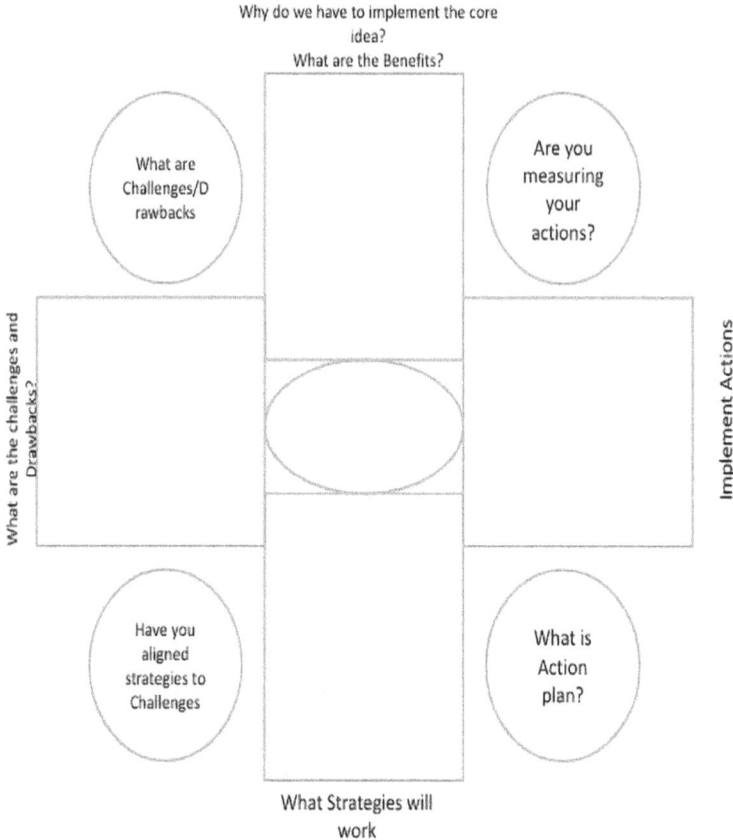

"Please scan to go to example"

Adaptability

Chapter 9
Selflessness

Every year, on the 5th of September, I have the privilege of celebrating Teacher's Day in India. It is a day dedicated to honouring the birth anniversary of the President of India, Sarvepalli Radhakrishnan. As a child, it meant a day off from school, but as I grew older, I began to deeply appreciate and respect our teachers.

The teaching profession is undoubtedly one of the noblest callings in the world. Teachers are like gardeners who plant countless seeds, knowing they may never sit in the shade of the trees they nurture. Their mantra is simple: give, give, and give some more. I have been fortunate to know many teachers in my family, and growing up in a small town, I have witnessed their dedication up close. Among all the people I have encountered, it is teachers whom I hold in the highest regard. They cultivate minds like forests, relish the beauty of knowledge, and start each day by entering the school gates at 8:25 AM.

Throughout my life, I have never seen teachers, be they from primary or high school, go on strikes, create disruptions, or disturb the harmony of their schools, cities, or states. Even in the face of inadequate facilities, limited amenities, or a lack of necessary equipment, they never waver in their commitment to educating future leaders.

In recent times, a friend of mine took it upon himself to adopt a school. He and his wife, both successful in the world of digital technology, made a conscious decision to return to their village and serve the children there. They stood shoulder to shoulder with selfless teachers, strategically transforming the school and giving back to the very community that had nurtured them years ago.

Nothing deters these educators from their mission. They face no problems with their students, never hesitate to teach a concept a second time, and are always impeccably prepared. In their days, there were no Key Performance Indicators (KPIs) or Key Result Areas (KRAs). They had the freedom to care for their students in their unique ways.

> *"A candle loses nothing by lighting another candle."*
> — James Keller

Teachers seldom experience promotions or the option to change their path. They are usually bound by a school or community and strive to be the best they can be. Some are strict, some sociable, and some process-oriented, but they all share one common trait: consistency. They ensure that the knowledge they impart stays with their students forever, whether it is multiplication tables or the periodic table.

Let me share the story of a close friend, a teacher who became an acting principal in a rural public school in Karnataka, India. He dreamt of seeing at least one medical student and a few engineers come from his school. Despite minimal facilities, he embarked on a journey of transformation. He reached out to friends, secured computers for the school, collaborated with organisations to provide sewing machines for students interested in vocational skills, and started vocational training with the limited resources available. He did not focus on a single grand dream; he aimed to provide a bright future for all his students. After seven years of consistent efforts, his hard work bore fruit. I do not think he was happier even when his own son secured an engineering seat. When he called me to share the achievements of his students, his voice quivered with emotion, and I knew tears filled his eyes. His commitment remained unshaken, and he raised the bar for himself, his staff, and his students. He continues to work tirelessly to fulfil the dreams of underprivileged families in the school's vicinity.

In these examples, we find two individuals committed to a cause greater than themselves. One was an engineer and entrepreneur who became a teacher, while the other was a dedicated career teacher. They could have pursued their personal success and financial gain, but they chose to invest in the school and its students. They realised that true fulfilment came from planting the seeds of knowledge and knowing they might never sit in the shade of the trees that would grow.

Their commitment transformed an ordinary public school into a thriving institution. They engaged the community and garnered support from students, parents, and staff. Their legacy

Selflessness

of selflessness, consistency, and commitment lives on in the hearts of thousands of students.

What can we learn from these remarkable educators, and how can we contribute to our communities?

> "Real education should educate us out of self into something far finer into a selflessness which links us with all humanity."
>
> Nancy Astor

Selflessness: Once I asked one of my leaders, "Sir, how come you are so nice to people and help as many as possible, share all the knowledge without holding back?" The answer to that was, my manager was nice to me because of him, I am what I am today, so I am following his principle. When we are in leadership positions and help people around us, the impact is not just on one person; it is on the generation of leaders who get motivated and continue the tradition of being selfless and sharing. Regardless of our position, we can give back, we can begin mentoring and coaching our teams or people who might benefit. Share your knowledge generously, provide strength, mentor, and build confidence in others. Let them know they have the potential to achieve their goals and be there for them when they need us. It is such a noble cause to share what we know. We are making a difference to a small community today; it will become big and revolutionise selfless giving.

Consistency: Nothing happens if something is done once. There needs to be continuity and consistency in approach. All the routines need to be done constantly as if it is a complicated requirement. Making consistency a way of life is much more fulfilling than forcefully incorporating it into our routine. Enjoy the continuity and consistency, and you will start seeing the differences. While we are selfless and share all that we have, we also need to establish routines, regularly check on people's progress and goals, and actively support their success. Do not waver; maintain your commitment to helping others. It is a learning game that every time we share something with someone, we also learn from that person. There is something to learn for us too.

Commitment: Doing anything for the first time is easy, or sharing randomly is also fine. Will they give any results? Maybe not. One of the approaches will not work for us or for the other person. We need to commit to the cause and sign up from the bottom of the heart for the purpose, then the magic happens. In our pursuit of creating a better world, let us lead others toward prosperity and happiness, this needs commitment. Time is one of the most valuable resources we have; once it is gone, it will not come back. Committing some of our time and resources to causes that matter is essential. The investment you make in others today will yield rich dividends in the future.

As we contemplate the legacy we will leave behind, remember that regrets on your deathbed come from missed opportunities to help your neighbours, friends, or teams. Give generously of your knowledge, time, kindness, love, and physical effort. You will spend the rest of your life basking in the warmth of cherished memories.

On Teacher's Day, reach out to your teachers, express your gratitude, and remember the invaluable role they played in your life. They may not remember you individually, but the impact they have had on your growth and development is immeasurable. Thank them every year; it costs nothing. And if you have the chance, visit them. If they are of my generation, they may not be on social media, but they will have a permanent address at the school. Seek them out and share the love and affection they so richly deserve.

Let us be like these teachers, planting saplings of positive change, knowing that we may never sit in the shade they provide. Through selflessness, consistency, and commitment, we can leave an enduring legacy that touches the lives of many.

This Story is inspired by Gowda, Sathish and Vijaya Miss

Exercise: Build your own selflessness model.

Worksheet

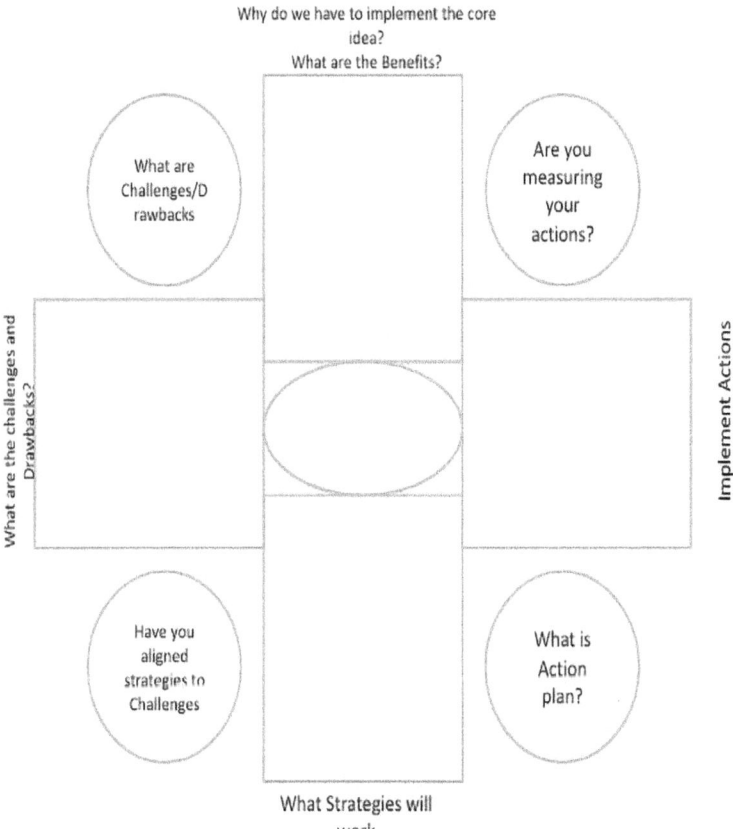

"Please scan to go to example"

Selflessness

Chapter 10
Imposter Syndrome

My career has been a diverse journey, spanning various roles and even different countries. As a software professional, I had always aspired to work on-site, closer to clients, in their offices, and in their countries. Such assignments were considered prestigious, with elevated levels of responsibility, acting as a crucial link between clients and delivery teams back in India. An on-site assignment was not only a badge of honour but also an embellishment on one's career profile. However, as is common in any software career, I found myself grappling with imposter syndrome during the periods between projects, especially when I was chosen for these coveted roles. I began attributing my success to mere luck. There were times when I started doubting my own abilities, particularly when tasks went unappreciated or were underappreciated, even when they were not meant to be monumental. My pursuit of perfection, along with success, left me feeling like a failure whenever I fell short, intensifying the imposter syndrome's grip on my self-esteem.

I placed an undue importance on external validation and endorsement as the sole benchmarks of success. Anything less felt like a reflection of my inadequacy, further fuelling my self-doubt. This constant cycle of self-sabotage confined me, limiting my exploration of new challenges and eroding my confidence.

In my struggle to overcome imposter syndrome, I found inspiration in the experiences of Tom Hanks, the renowned multiple Academy Award winner. He, too, confessed to moments when he felt like an imposter in the film industry, believing that he did not deserve the accolades he earned. His remedy was to take on more challenging roles, appreciating that film success was the result of collaborative teamwork and dedication. With consistent perseverance, he managed to confront and conquer imposter syndrome.

> "Perfectionism and imposter syndrome often go hand in hand, and this is the most common type of imposter."
> – Dr Jessamy Hibberd

While opportunities are often associated with luck and I considered luck played a significant role in my life, delving into the unexpected and unplanned opportunities and succeeding in them is a testimony enough that I was not incompetent. My successes were not easy to achieve, often I was disillusioned due to the limited knowledge of the domain of the opportunity from career to family to health and relations. And the pillar of my strength has been my wife, who not only encouraged a step forward but also ushered my perspective into the bright side of failure, the experience of exploring the lands and cultures anew.

One of the ways of self-motivation is by constantly reminding myself of the ancient explorers and their perilous voyages over deep waters into the abyss of the unknown whose perseverance to discover new lands, new trade routes with just the stars as their navigation. Undertaking the unknown itself is a brave act and when the risks are affordable, an opportunity qualifies its worth to attempt. While my assignments I undertook are puny and unworthy of comparison to the pioneers of yore, I draw an inspiration to lift my spirits upon extrapolating to contemporary relevance. In my own way these motivations kept me afloat from branding myself as an imposter.

As a family we prepped each other to face the consequences of failure juxtaposed with the excitement of the adventure. We presented a worst-case scenario to ourselves across the important facets of our life of schooling, career, relations, health and how failure would impact our future. Even as there were more unknowns, we stood by each other as a unit and the decision was always taken as a family. Hence, our achievements are legitimately achieved by engaging with risk and unquantifiable sacrifices.

Over time, I came to appreciate the vital role my family played in helping me confront my self-doubt and fears. They reminded me of my numerous successes and why I was selected for these coveted assignments. Even with a quarter-century of experience behind me, I still turn to my family for guidance in accepting my vulnerabilities, imperfections, and shortcomings. Most importantly, I learned that success need not be perfect every time.

I have learned to coexist with imposter syndrome, approaching opportunities with the mindset that I may not always be perfect, but I possess the skills needed for success. My journey underscores the importance of self-awareness and the support of loved ones in conquering imposter syndrome, ultimately allowing us to reach our full potential and embrace new challenges with confidence. Every one of us is unique and purposeful. Let us get over the feelings of inadequacy and self-doubt, focus on our strengths, believe in ourselves, celebrate our achievements, and seek help from our family and well-wishers to overcome this hurdle.

Imposter Syndrome is the inability to believe that one's success is deserved or has been legitimately achieved as a result of one's own effort or skills. This syndrome is associated with perfectionism and occurs when you feel that you have not given your absolute best to the task at hand, leading to feelings of incompetence.

Exercise: Build your own model to get over imposter syndrome.

Worksheet.

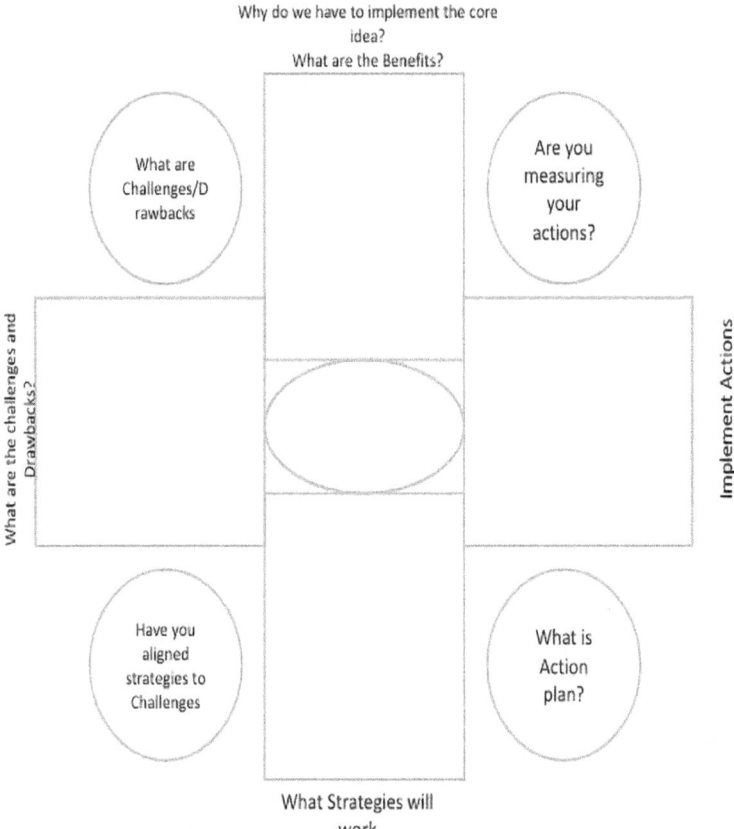

"Please scan to go to example"

Imposter Syndrome

Chapter 11
Don't Live with Regret

In the heart of a quaint village, my father, a man of modest dreams, came into this world, much like me. Born into a family of diligent farmers, he nurtured dreams beyond the boundaries of our humble fields. His education journey carried him through the 11th grade, yet circumstances and an unwavering commitment to serve his nation led him to a different path - he enlisted in the army. This path led him to the front lines during the Indo-Bangladesh war and found him steadfastly supporting troops during the tumultuous India-Pakistan conflict. Following his honourable retirement, he returned to the comforting embrace of our village, dedicating his life to family, and witnessing our growth.

As the years advanced, he frequently spoke of his dreams – dreams to venture Delhi, to pay homage at the memorials of revered leaders, and to witness the breathtaking grandeur of the Taj Mahal in Agra. These dreams, brimming with significance, remained suspended in the air, always on the horizon but never truly grasped. In hindsight, we, his children, failed to fully comprehend the weight of those dreams during his lifetime.

Then, one fateful day, an unforgiving stroke and heart attack took him from us. It was at that moment we realised the profound significance of those unfulfilled dreams. His simple wish, once suspended in the air, remained forever out of reach.

My mother harboured a different dream, one that centred on the ethereal beauty of snow. When she visited New Zealand, we made plans to traverse the snowy landscapes. Yet, just as we were on the brink of this long-awaited journey, an unexpected illness struck me, rendering me incapacitated and unable to navigate the winding, snow-covered roads. Days turned into weeks, and though we contemplated going, we hesitated, and eventually, she returned to her homeland, her dream of seeing and stepping on snow was unfulfilled. She journeyed to the Holy Land, explored the vibrant streets of Singapore, and marvelled at the beauty of New Zealand, but her explorations within India were limited. Her yearning for travel remained stifled by circumstances and time.

It was only when she received the grim diagnosis of advanced-stage kidney cancer that we, as a family, seriously considered a trip to Shimla to capture her dream of snow. Sadly, her health deteriorated at an alarming pace, rendering the journey an impossible feat.

Two cherished family members carried with them simple desires that I, their kin, could not bring to fruition. Their unfulfilled dreams haunt me to this very day, even though my father's passing occurred 22 years ago and my mother's five years ago. The question continues to linger: why didn't I grasp those fleeting opportunities when they stood before me?

For countless years, I have carried this burden of regret, and it appears as though it will forever shadow my existence. We all know that we cannot rewrite the past; however, we have the power to reshape our future. Living not in regret but actively learning from our experiences is the key, as each lesson becomes a stepping stone toward a more enlightened and fulfilling journey ahead. This transformation requires a closer and mindful examination of how we deal with situations. Drawing from my own experience in overcoming regret, I found that empathy and removing delayed gratification played crucial roles in adopting a more positive perspective towards life.

> "Accept your past without regret, handle your present with confidence and your future without fear."
> — Dr. APJ Abdul Kalam

The illustrious French Renaissance essayist and philosopher, Michel de Montaigne, once wrote about living life to the fullest, which includes refraining from dwelling on past mistakes. In an essay titled, "On Repentance," he candidly expressed, "I have generally only myself to blame for my errors or mistakes… For my grief is soothed by the reflection that things were bound to happen as they did." He believed that every choice we make, including those leading to feelings of wasted time, moulds us into the individuals we become. Regrets, like milestones, mark our unique life journeys.

Reflecting on the narrative of my own life and the experiences of those I have encountered, I have come to realise the paramount importance of confronting regret. To live without regrets, I have embraced a set of strategies:

Embrace the Present: All too often, we are quick to delay actions, postponing our personal pursuits. I vividly remember the pivotal moment when my coach posed a question: "What are your priorities?" Shockingly, I had not placed self-care anywhere near the top of my list. The coach's following query was equally profound: "How much do you invest in yourself, both in terms of time and resources?" To my dismay, I found myself at a loss for an answer. It was a moment of reckoning. I had neglected my own well-being, placing family responsibilities at the forefront, with my career a close second. It was then, as I sat gazing at the South Pacific waves caressing the shore, that the revelation struck. I could not resist picking up the phone to call my coach and express my gratitude. The transformation was palpable.

My priorities shifted, my self-worth received the attention it deserved, and my approach to life was forever altered. I now assert with confidence that I can care for my clients as capable as I care for myself and my family. This personal journey taught me a fundamental lesson: when opportunities arise in our personal and professional lives, seize them without hesitation. Whether it is attending to the needs of family or nurturing your own well-being, do it without delay. Shed self-doubt, and permit others to recognise your capabilities.

Take the First Step: The wisdom of Lao Tzu resonates powerfully: "The journey of a thousand miles begins with one step." This serves as an inspiring reminder to take that initial step, no matter the daunting obstacles that loom on the path ahead. We often carry the baggage of stigma, fear of failure, the unknown, and the inertia that keeps us rooted. I recall my own apprehension when I embarked on a journey to conquer my fitness goals. The thought of a 2-3-minute stint on the cross trainer at the gym seemed overwhelming. Yet, I decided to take that first step and began walking. In a week's time, I had clocked five kilometres in an hour and soon aimed for 10 kilometres. Six months later, I was breezing through ten kilometres in just 90 minutes. The turning point came when I registered for a half marathon and achieved a personal best of 3 hours and 20 minutes. The individual who had once feared a mere 2-kilometre walk was now conquering a half marathon. My secret? Action. It is the key to success. Today, I make no mistakes when it comes to family. I act swiftly on their needs, leaving no room for regret. Instead of wondering what could have been, I revel in what I have accomplished, even if it was through failure. I am content, and my family thrives.

Confront Challenges Head-On: Life often presents us with challenges, and our attitude towards facing them can either stifle our growth or fuel our resilience. It is not about taking on every challenge that comes your way but about wisely choosing your battles. Each challenge should be a calculated risk, not a reckless endeavour. There is a thin line between arrogance and assertiveness, and it is crucial to adopt an assertive approach when confronting challenges. Preparation, strategy, approach, and readiness for consequences are key. Not every battle will result in victory, but each encounter teaches us invaluable lessons about facing adversity and reveals the extent of our preparedness. Running from challenges will not lead to personal growth. To truly grow, we must embrace challenges with conviction, and even in defeat, we gain knowledge that will guide us toward future triumphs.

Addressing regret head-on allows us to lead a more harmonious life. Our quality of life improves, and as we approach the final chapter of our journey, we can rest assured that we lived with purpose and to the fullest. Regrets need not be our constant companions.

In the simplest terms, we must act, when necessary, support others always, engage in meaningful conversations, laugh, cry, and savour the company of those who share our journey. After all, we are human beings, living in interconnected tribes. Some may say, "Live life king size," but for me, the essence lies in living a life that is both serene and eventful. We should gather stories to pass on to our children and grandchildren, stories that inspire them to embrace the present and banish the spectre of regret. And hoping this one will achieve that objective.

Exercise: Build your own model to win on regret.

Worksheet

"Please scan to go to example"

Don't Live with Regret

Chapter 12
Embracing Life's Golden Opportunities

In continuation to our earlier chapter, "Don't live with Regret," we delve into an imperative need to seize opportunities by connecting the dots from our past, fostering the groundwork for a brilliant future.

Life unfolds before us, offering invaluable opportunities waiting to be seized, fostering our dreams. In the backdrop of unwavering support from loved ones, friends, and family, these opportunities promise profound happiness and the chance to enrich our lives remarkably. However, many of us hesitate, uncertain whether to seize them or let life's treasures slip through our fingers due to indecision.

As the ancient Chinese philosopher, Lao Tzu, wisely proclaimed, "The journey of a thousand miles begins with one step," the essence of progress lies in that initial step, the catalyst for transformation.

Hesitation, that initial reluctance akin to a car with a dead battery, paralyses our progress. Rather than abandoning the car, we seek assistance to set the wheels in motion, just as in life, where seizing opportunities hinges on that first vital decision - a choice that sparks the engine of transformation.

Adopting Discipline and relinquishing our fear of failure, seeking help propels us towards the journey we aspire to undertake. By evaluating problems and generating myriad potential solutions, accountable only to us, we find that practical solutions, often simple, lead us toward a better, refined version of ourselves.

Taking the initial step towards change brings us one step closer to our destiny. My journey, commencing in a quaint village surrounded by unpretentious farmers, revealed life's simple approaches to challenges. Growing up in a village where even basic amenities like shops and restaurants were absent, our perspectives were uncomplicated, and the sense of community extended beyond individual families. Despite the simplicity of this life, one fear loomed large in my mind - a fear of water.

In our village, learning to swim took place in open wells, lakes, and water streams. Despite numerous attempts by my father to teach me, my resistance persisted. An elderly gentleman passing by one summer vacation inquired about my reluctance. Upon learning of my fear, he chose not to judge but to enlighten. Swimming, he explained, was a life skill, reinforcing advice from my father and grandfather with compelling examples. Generously offering to teach me, I agreed under the condition that he stayed by my side. That day, he became my guiding light, helping me overcome my fear of water. Since that pivotal moment, swimming has become an integral part of my life.

Open well similar to the one I learnt swimming.

My decision to conquer this fear filled my parents and younger brother with pride. Had I hesitated that day and refrained from saying "yes," I might never have learned to swim fearlessly. This underscores the immense impact one decision can have on our lives.

In the grand journey of life, effective decision-making plays a pivotal role in shaping our futures, both personally and professionally. Challenges and a wavering motivation are inevitable, yet nothing is permanent. "We have explored human-centric uncertainties and drawbacks in earlier chapters to find simple solutions. Sometimes, forsaking a familiar path is necessary to forge ahead towards our intended destination. A beautiful ending does not signify the end of the world; instead, it often ushers in something far better than we could have imagined.

> "Life is not about waiting for the storm to pass but learning to dance in the rain."
> – Vivian Greene

I urge each one of us to draw inspiration from these words and keep moving forward, echoing Denzel Washington, who once said, "Fall forward." Even stumbling signifies progress, providing clarity on what we are up against. We are vulnerable, our methods might oppose our needs, yet we can explore new methods resonating with our mindset and unique needs. Each individual faces distinct challenges, operates at their own level, and delves into varying depths. Navigating uncharted waters requires a deep dive, seeking fundamental understanding and applying simple solutions that may not be easy but are undoubtedly effective.

The change we make in ourselves remains incomplete until its impact is visible and recognised by those around us.

While changing ourselves is relatively easy, changing others' perceptions is more arduous. The world around us changes when we change, their approach changes, and so do their opinions. Small incremental shifts create substantial impacts in the greater journey of life.

In the journey of life, our primary focus is often to become better human beings. Is there a necessity to be unconditionally good to others in a world teeming with challenges and competition? The answers to these questions are as varied as the people who seek them. Every situation is unique, and the application of these principles differs with each individual. Based on our experiences, we string together a model to address a situation and derive your own approach to handle it. With unwavering confidence, I can assert that implementing the model, practising the strategies, and applying them diligently will not lead to regression in our lives. The only path we will tread upon is one of continuous improvement.

I implore you to make a conscious effort to become the best version of yourselves and strive for excellence. Life's promise propels us forward in a world that is ever-changing. Embrace challenges and seek progress, for each day's end signals a new beginning, rich with potential and opportunity. Internalise and apply these words, for therein lies the path to a life well-lived.

In our bonus chapter, we articulate a real example of a leader who worked on his anger. This serves as great motivation, demonstrating that the model worked and can be adopted to improve in the chosen path. We are eager to listen to your journey and strategies you would like to share. With your permission, we offer to bring your stories to life through our blogs and social media as advocates for Simplexity.

Bonus Chapter
A Journey from Chaos to Control

In the early chapters of my life, I wore the label of an "angry young man" like a badge. It defined me, shaping my actions into a pattern of rudeness, aggression, and loudness. I was bossy, prone to fights, and had few friends. Conversations with me were futile, as my argumentative nature pushed people away.

One particularly dark incident during my engineering days stands out vividly. In a fit of rage, I punched someone in the face at a theatre for revealing a movie's plot. The repercussions could have been severe – broken teeth and a bleeding mouth. The spectre of legal consequences loomed, threatening to land me in jail.

Another episode, involving a road rage incident with a truck driver, nearly cost me my life. In a moment of blind fury, I overtook the truck, applied the brakes, and stopped my bike. Miraculously, the truck halted as well. It was a wake-up call to my dangerous behaviour.

Life took an unexpected turn when my job demanded extensive travel across the country, averaging 20 days a month. This marked the beginning of my transformative journey. Meeting a diverse array of individuals during my constant travels exposed me to the richness of life – from the affluent to the impoverished, the violent to the defensive, the unethical to the saintly.

As my perspective evolved, those around me noticed a change. Encouragement replaced avoidance, and I began to realise the profound impact of gaining control over my anger. Unbeknownst to me at the time, I adopted various strategies without a formal model. Looking back, my exploration and experiences were following a transformation model that I experimented many years later. The Simplexity Transformation Model will help in assisting in finding simple solutions for complex problems.

In those days, there were no measurement tools; reactions were gauged from people's responses. Today, we give you a Simplexity Transformation Traceability Matrix (STTM), a powerful tool to track action plans for each challenge and strategy. My journey, once marked by chaos and aggression, has become a testament to the transformative power of controlling anger, with the diverse characters I encountered along the way adding depth and colour to the narrative.

Here is the model for Anger transformation matrix and its corresponding Transformation Traceability Matrix(STTM) used to track the identified actions.

```
                    Why should I work on my Anger?
                    What are the benefits?

    ┌─────────┐                              ┌─────────┐
    │ What are│                              │ Are you │
    │ Challeng│                              │measurin │
    │es/Drawb │                              │ g your  │
    │  acks   │                              │actions? │
    └─────────┘                              └─────────┘

 What are the                                              Implement
 challenges and          ╔═════════╗                       Actions
 Drawbacks I had         ║  Anger  ║
                         ╚═════════╝

    ┌─────────┐                              ┌─────────┐
    │Have you │                              │         │
    │ aligned │                              │ What is │
    │strategie│                              │ Action  │
    │   s to  │                              │  plan?  │
    │ Challeng│                              │         │
    │   es    │                              │         │
    └─────────┘                              └─────────┘

                    Which Strategies will
                         work?
```

Anger Transformation Model

"Please scan to go to example"

A Journey from Chaos to Control

#	Benefits(Customer & Personal)	Drawback/Challenges	Strategies	Action Items
1				

Simplexity Transformation Traceability Matrix

Now, when people question whether I ever get angry, my response is a candid "yes." The difference lies in how I process that anger and manage to wear a smile through it. Road rage, once a perilous battlefield, no longer elicits a fiery response from me. I

"Please scan to go to example"

have learned not to carry someone else's baggage.

The journey from unbridled anger to self-mastery has not eradicated the emotion but has bestowed upon me the wisdom to navigate its currents. Now, anger is a transient visitor, passing through without leaving a destructive mark. Through this metamorphosis, I have discovered the strength to face challenges with composure and emerge on the other side with a genuine smile.

One Benefit can have multiple Drawbacks, pickup best suited one. In case strategies, there can be Strategies to address one drawback, list them all and duplicates can have different action items. Some action items can overlap that give the same result. Once we have an action plan, we need to have a tracking strategy. Build a tracking mechanism that suits and measures the progress every week. Some you may have executed daily and some as planned.

Measuring results

This model operates based on outcomes resembling the following: If we discontinue after a certain period, both our perception and proficiency decline below the initial point, impacting the consistency we convey to those in our vicinity.

Feel free to talk to us if you need more information on how to build and track the STM, STTM, Action plans and measuring results.

STM → STTM + Action plan + Measuring results
References
- Brene Brown's works
- Simon Sinek's works
- MGSCC: Marshall Goldsmith's Works

- Harvard Business school
- https://www.oprahdaily.com/life/a39078306/oprah-the-life-you-want-vulnerability-class/
- https://www.psychologytoday.com/us/blog/think-act-be/201911/5-simple-ways-manage-stress-and-anxiety-every-day
- https://www.psychologytoday.com/us/blog/think-act-be/202008/5-proven-ways-relieve-covid-related-depression